THE DIVINE MOTHER

TEACHINGS OF
THE ORDER OF CHRISTIAN MYSTICS

THE DIVINE MOTHER

THE DIVINE MOTHER

Transcribed by
HARRIETTE AUGUSTA CURTISS
and
F. HOMER CURTISS, B.S., M.D.
Founders of
THE ORDER OF CHRISTIAN MYSTICS
and
AUTHORS OF THE "CURTISS BOOKS"

2012 EDITION

REPUBLISHED FOR THE ORDER BY
MOUNT LINDEN PUBLISHING
JOHANNESBURG, SOUTH AFRICA
ISBN: 978-1-920483-06-7

Dedication

This edition is lovingly dedicated to the Memory

of the Founders of

The Order of Christian Mystics

Pyrahmos and Rahmea

and to

The Teacher of the Order

who on earth was called

Helena Petrovna Blavatsky

"Ministers of Christ and Stewards of the Mysteries of God."

1 Corinthians 4 vs. 1

"The point is transformed into a diameter. It now symbolizes a divine immaculate Mother-Nature within the all-embracing absolute Infinitude." – *The Secret Doctrine*, Blavatsky, I, 34.

CONTENTS

FOREWORD

WHAT child of Earth ever lived who has not dreamed dreams of a great and wonderful gift to be miraculously bestowed? And generally these dreams have included the idea of a great feast, of a dainty and delicious repast far out of the ordinary. As we grow to manhood and womanhood our longing dreams take on a more mystical character and we try to feed them on the literal story of a Christ-child born of Mary and laid in a manger, a Child who shall bring to the world "Peace, good will toward men." But, alas, we still await that peace, our hunger unassuaged, our gift and feast seemingly still but a dream.

In this little booklet there comes, not to those who are satisfied, but to all who still feel the great yearning for the gift of gifts to man, who still feel the unassuaged longing for something outside of and greater than the outer gifts so bounteously bestowed by the Father, who feel stirring within the Womb of the New Age a life-force so potent, a consciousness so inspiring that they ask: Can this be the herald of the long promised Babe symbolized in song and story? destined at last to fulfill all prophecies, as no babe born of human parents has ever more than symbolized? Is this wonderful Presence to be the Child of the New Age, of whom it can truly be said: "That holy thing. . . . shall be called the Son of God?"

Today, as never before, a cry of heart-hunger goes up from a humanity which has waited so long for a real understanding of all that, age after age, it has accepted, has striven to live for, has died for, yet has not fully understood or received. This great hunger-cry is not a cry for physical things but is the fulfillment of the days so long foretold of old: "Behold, the days come, saith the Lord God, that I will send a famine in the land, not a famine of bread, nor a thirst for water, but of hearing the words of the Lord."

Therefore, in response to the great need of Her children, the Divine Mother comes today and finds that Her children have grown up, have reached the age when they feel that they must put away childish things, can no longer be entertained by or accept mere wonder-tales, but must be given the opportunity to analyze and understand, yet their hearts still yearn for the Christmas greeting from their Divine Mother and they are eager to partake of the bounteously spread feast of spiritual food She has prepared for them.

To all such the Divine Mother comes holding in her outstretched arms the radiant form of Her Son, the Lord of Glory, the fruit of Her bringing forth. With the birth of Her Son in this New Age, She brings to our remembrance all that has been told us, all that has been whispered to our hearts during the dark watches of the long night, all that the Light has revealed in the mystical depths of our consciousness. And in Her loving voice, soft as the whisper of a gentle air from heaven, She says: "Children, behold my Son!" And She beckons to the heart-hungry and says: "Welcome to my feast. It is spread for all who will come and partake and live." "For the bread of God is he which cometh down from heaven, and giveth life to the world."[*]

San Francisco, November 15th, 1921.

---

[*] *St. John*, VI, 33.

THE DIVINE MOTHER

"The Great Mother holds out her arms to all her children, be they Pagan, Jew, Christian or non-Christian, recognizing that each child must feed at its mother's breast and partake of the milk of her love and sympathy, no matter what the circumstances of his or her physical life, or what their religious training." *The Voice of Isis*, Curtiss, 28.

"Realize Sakti as your Mother Divine; your spirit's worshipful Queen Mother in your heart of hearts, as your innermost Self— Listen to the voice of Sakti in the temple of your heart." *Kalpaka Magazine*, February 1920, 55.

"In the beginning God created the heaven and the earth. And the earth was without form and void; and darkness was upon the face of the deep. And the Spirit of God moved upon the face of the waters. . . . And God said, Let there be a firmament in the midst of the waters, and let it divide the waters from the waters." *Genesis*, I, 1, 2, 6.

IN the few graphic words quoted at the head of this chapter the *Bible* suggests rather than describes the beginnings of this planet, Earth. In the beginning the heavens and the earth were not differentiated and hence could well be symbolized by a circle, containing in its formless void all things in potentiality. It

was covered with a vast darkness in which
the future habitation of man incubated,
much as a mother bird covers her nest,
shutting out every glimmer of light from
the unborn nestlings, lest the development
of the germs of life hidden within them
should be aborted. But just as the mother
bird could not bring forth life in eggs
not fertilized by the father bird so that
the inert fluids within were coagulated
and transmuted into individual forms of
sentient life, neither could the Waters of
Life or the Great Deep bring forth until it
had been fructified by the Spirit of God
moving silently yet potently over the
Waters of Chaos.

Out of the brooding darkness came
the firmament* which divided the waters
of Universal Space, or the formless void
of mere potentiality, from the specialized
Waters of Manifestation, within which
our globe was incubated like a cosmic
egg from which the Spirit of God was to
be expressed within the limitations of the
specialized forms of life which were to be
brought forth. This stage of development,
be it in planet, man or chick, can be symbolized by a circle with a horizontal line — the
firmament drawn through its center, just
as the mother bird makes a firmament

(*) See *The Voice of Isis*, Curtiss, 321-2.

separating the vastness of the world at large from the miniature world within the egg in which the coming manifestation is to be segregated and secluded.

The great Divine Mother is not something apart from God, but a definite and necessary manifestation or expression of God as Divine Love. It is from this eternal truth that all great religions have recognized and immortalized the Mother-aspect of the Divine as co-equal with the Father-aspect, altho among Christians the Catholic Church is the only one which emphasizes or gives much attention to it, and then only as the materialized and limited human mother of the personalized man, Jesus. "Thus we have *Mary*, the mother of Jesus; *Myrrha*, mother of Bacchus; *Mair*, mother of Hermes; *Maya Maria*, mother of the Siamese Savior, Sommona Cadom; *Myrrha*, mother of the Greek Adonis; *Maya*, mother of Agni; *Maya*, mother of Buddha; *Miriam*, the prophetess—mother of Israel; *Mizram*, mother of Joshua; *Minerva*, the Virgin Queen,"[*] and so forth.

In various philosophies there are many other names for the Divine Mother which indicate some of her attributes, such as the "Mother of Mercy and Knowledge,"

---

[*] *The Key of Destiny*, Curtiss, 145.

"the Mother (fire), the Wife (water), and
the Daughter (air) of the Logos"; Shakti,
the energy of the Essence of the Father,
Son and Holy Ghost. "It is also called
Mulaprakriti (the root of Nature), also
Electricity, both seen and unrevealed." She
is also called "the Divine Voice"; "God
spake the Word and we were made." She
is also called "Akasha, the synthesis of all
the forces of Nature and of all the magic
potencies of Occult Sound in Nature and
in Ether," the gentle cooing or chirping
of the mother bird calling to her young;
also that which we call the Soundless
Sound, the inarticulate sound or voice of
the bursting bud, the growing grain, the
whisper of unseen waters.

Back of all such universal myths and al-
legories there must be and is a divine truth,
for truth is sensed by all sincere aspirants
who seek to penetrate into the mysteries
of life. Hence, all who seek of God for
ultimate truth, find this Mother-aspect
revealed to them personally and also expressed in various ways in all religions.
Therefore, let us also strive to realize the
truth back of this universal idea.

We are told that "God is love" and
love is the feminine attribute or expression of God through which all things

are brought forth. "The Mother of humanity is that mighty Passive Principle which gathers up the Light as it penetrates Chaos and cherishes it in her bosom. It is forever the tender, brooding Mother-force which works on the germs of good in all things that they may ultimately bring forth that good. It is that unseen Mother-love of the Godhead hovering like a dove over its nestling, which feeds with "food convenient for us" every hungry heart, even if that food be seemingly bitter to the taste; that unseen agency which, when the fury of the tempest has spent itself and the Sun shines forth, brings out its purifying effects."[*]

It is the Water of Life poured forth by the Man or Water-bearer in the Sign Aquarius, this sign thus typifying the dual aspect of creation: God the Father (the Man) wills to pour forth the Great Creative Force as Love (water) which becomes the Mother of all things, and which brings forth in man the Son or the Light of the Christ-consciousness, that Light "which lighteth every man that cometh into the world"; that mystic Light which makes both life and love manifest definitely. All life manifests as Light, hence on Earth all living things

---

[*] *The Key to the Universe*, Curtiss, 192-3.

give forth a form of light-rays
(radioactivity) or have an aura which will
affect a properly prepared photographic
plate.

The Divine Mother is the Bringer
Forth and Sustainer of the universe,
the Comforter whom Jesus promised to
leave with us, "even unto the end," that it
might bring all things to our remembrance
whatsoever He has told us. For only as
the Divine Mother comforts Her children
and brings to their remembrance the realization of their essential divinity as "Sons
of God and heirs to His kingdom"; brings
joy out of sorrow and wisdom out of error,
can She bring forth in them the perfect
expression of their Real (Divine) Selves.

Among the Hindus one aspect of
the Divine Mother is recognized under the name of Sakti. "Realize Sakti as
your Mother Divine. . . . A student of
Kayasiddhi lives in Sakti, moves in Sakti
and has his being in Sakti. . . . The student feels that he is always and forever
in the presence of Sakti. . . . That he can
cause Sakti to feel him, love him, seek
him, want him, find him. . . . Sakti is everywhere. Simply let Sakti have her way.
Do not resist. Let not your doubt or despair or lack of faith stand between you
and Sakti. . . .

Live in the thought that Sakti loves you—
the Universal One from whom are all
forces and all things."[*]

In the first chapter of *Genesis* we
read that at first: "God created man in
his own image, in the image of God created he him; male and female created he
them"—i.e., androgynous. And it was only
far later in evolution, when "the heavens
and the earth were finished, and all the
host of them," that this spiritual Race descended into physical embodiment in the
second symbolic Adam made of the dust
of the Earth. Then a deep sleep (the night
period between the Races)[**] overtook the
consciousness of that divine androgynous,
ethereal and semi-astral Race, during
which, coming under the Law of Duality
which rules all physical manifestation,
the Passive Principle or Love-nature was
individualized and separated as a rib and
embodied as Eve, the first physical mother.

Thus at the dawn of the next great
stage of evolution the male and female
aspects of the Spiritual Man found themselves separated, yet working together
to express the whole; the masculine
aspect as will, logic, courage, pro-

[*] The *Kalpaka Magazine*, February, 1920, 54-5.
[**] See *The Voice of Isis*, Curtiss, Chapter XVII.

jective, fructifying consciousness and
physical power; the feminine aspect as the
brooding love, tenderness, compassion,
spiritual power and the ability to bring
forth and nourish that which has been
fructified.

And only by the perfect union of these
two Principles can "the Christ be born in
you." Like St. Paul, we must all travail in
the birth pangs, together with all creation,
until this divine spiritual birth takes place,
first within us individually, then in all humanity. It is therefore this feminine aspect
of the Godhead, the Divine Mother-aspect
and its power to bring forth in us, which
we will consider in this little volume.

It is said by some that "God thought
and his thoughts brought forth the universe." But this is only a half truth, for
only as thought is united with and vital-
ized by emotion can it bring forth the
idea into manifestation. Also, every vital
thought brings forth a thrill of emotion.
Hence, God's thought, united to Divine
Love, which gave it the power to manifest, filled all space and brought forth after
the pattern of the ideal projected from the
Divine Mind.

Again, we are often told that God
breathed out from His own Being all
the manifested worlds. This is also

true, for the breath contains both the Father and Mother-forces, heat and moisture. Hence, that Divine Breath, containing the all-embracing Love, brings forth the universe in perfection, harmony and beauty, embodying within it everything needed for the evolution, comfort, health and happiness of the as yet unborn races of men.

If this realization could be brought more fully to our consciousness and, instead of merely breathing automatically to sustain life like the animals, we mentally invoked and correlated with the Divine Mother-force through the breath, we could bring forth according to our purified will. It is therefore important that the breath be kept pure and sweet. It is the purifier of the body as well as the sustainer of life; hence, if we permit it to be over-laden with an excess of bodily impurities it will hinder our correlation with the Divine Mother.

In Nature we often see an excess of either heat (masculine) or moisture (feminine), either of which retard growth. But then comes the wind (breath of heaven) as an equalizer between them. It blows gently or fiercely according to conditions, one of its functions being to equalize the heat and moisture as well as sweep away all foul odors. In man the breath has the same function of equalization. As a result of conditions which he has set up through his ignorance of and indifference to the Divine Law, the wind often becomes the agent of karmic equalization and adjustment—through storms and other destructive conditions—on Earth. But always the Divine Mother covers up the scars and renews the devastated regions with a mantle of verdure.

Just so the breath in man, because of his ignorance and indifference to the love of the Divine Mother, becomes polluted and hence brings inharmony instead of equalization to his body. Thus it becomes to man an agent of karmic readjustment through storms of sickness, poverty and unhappiness.

In each human being, as in each seed, the Father-Mother—heat and moisture— must be absorbed and united if growth is to take place. Undeveloped man uses these forces, like a seed dropped by the wayside, in a haphazard way, but if, through understanding, he unites the two scientifically, he brings forth like a highly cultivated seed that is protected, fertilized and cared for. The moisture-aspect of the Divine Mother will bring forth that Love in man, if he will but receive it, by which he can be led to the Wisdom of the Father.

Only the feminine aspect of God-consciousness could have expressed so much tender beauty and delicate charm, so much harmony and melody, or could have stored up in the bowels of the earth, in the depths of the sea and the heights of the air such boundless stores of health, wealth and happiness.

Only the foresight of Divine Mother-love could have filled the air with vitality to sustain life, and implanted in the minerals of the earth and the herbs of the field the differentiated life-essences which, when properly used under the law of sympathy or affinity, would restore harmony to every inharmony, health to every illness, and meet the needs of every disability which man, during his childhood of ignorance, was apt to bring upon himself.

A purely masculine aspect of consciousness we could readily think of as saying: "I have made all things perfect in form and function; have given to man the ability to correlate with the currents of life and health and wisdom and prosperity. Why, then, should I prepare in advance an antidote for his self-inflicted ills? Let him learn to obey the law."

But the great love-aspect, the Divine

Mother, realizing the results of man's childish ignorance and selfishness, prepared beforehand a balm for every ill, a lullaby for every sorrow, a comfort for every grief, and implanted in every heart an inner urge to respond to Her Love; to realize the tender watchful care that would not that any suffer; the inborn certainty in every heart that there is a way out of every difficulty, and a determination to find that way.

This Eternal Urge in each heart to return to its Divine Source, no matter how deeply sunk in matter or how lost in the darkness of ignorance, is brought forth by the surge of the mighty stream of Divine Love ever flowing back to its Source, carrying all its children with it.

All attraction and cohesion is a manifestation of Divine Love—the affinity of the protons and electrons which compose the atoms, the chemical attraction of the atoms which compose the molecules of matter, as well as the attraction that holds the planets in their orbits around the Sun, and the attraction that unites the individual Soul to God and draws it ever upward.

Love is also a master vibration. Hence only as that vibration flows through and finds expression in the various forms of life can their atoms hold together and manifest these forms; only as it flows through us can there be any real life in us. It is also harmony and rhythm. Hence only as we allow the currents of Divine Love to flow through us unimpeded and unresisted can we manifest harmony in our bodies or minds. This is the secret of both health and peace.

"Sakti (the Divine Mother) is in me; Sakti is in the universe, says the Mantra— Yogi. He simply *lets Her work* and does not stand between Herself and the Work. . . . 'Hers is the work—I am but a tool in Her all-powerful hands.'. . . Identifying himself *by devotion and self-surrender* with the Supreme Sakti, the Mantra-Yogi gives the command, couched in affirmative Mantra, and lets the Sakti in him work out the result."[*]

The process is not complicated, simply "grow as the flower grows," opening its heart to the warmth of the Sun and drinking in the dew of heaven. Complications seem to arise only when we strive to analyze and understand the details of the workings of the Law. It is a simple act to breathe, but a complicated act to understand, for to do so we must know the chemistry of the air and

---

[*] *The Kalpaka Magazine*, May 1920, 176.

the blood, as well as the complicated physiology and anatomy of respiration and circulation. But we can breathe and maintain perfect health without that technical knowledge. Just so we can correlate with the Divine Mother through love and learn to know God without a knowledge of the details of the process.

If we react to and express the lower vibrations which resist and counteract and shut out Love, such as anger, hatred, jealousy, resentment, revenge, envy, criticism, etc., the vibrations of harmony cannot manifest and hold the atoms together in rhythm, and our bodily functions are disturbed and illness or disease (inharmony) results. But since man is the "microcosm of the macrocosm" he can consciously correlate with the Divine Mother in thought and emotion and through love bring forth and manifest in his consciousness and in his very flesh the fruit of that perfect harmony which is his birthright.

"For God so loved the world, that he gave his only begotten Son, that whosoever believeth on him should not perish, but have everlasting life." The "only begotten Son" is the Cosmic Christ-principle or the One Divine Life-force, the Sun-force in Nature and the Son force in man. Only as we let the love of the Divine Mother surround, fill and manifest through us can we establish the state of harmony in which the Christ-life and consciousness can be born in us.

The great Master Jesus lived and moved and had his Being in this great stream of Divine Love and thus became a Christ as an example to us of how we also may have that same Christ-life and consciousness born in us. Jesus was the "first fruits" or culmination or perfect manifestation of this outpouring of the creative Will and Love (Father-Mother), and was the exemplar of the laws that must be followed and the attainment that must be reached by all mankind *in due season* before it can become one with its Father-Mother or reach the At-one-ment.

We can gain a new conception of the state of harmony we must ultimately manifest to reach this attainment if we divide the word atonement thus, a-tone-ment; that is, the tone that is meant to manifest; that key-note of Divine Harmony which is now being manifested by our Higher Self and which is striving to make us respond to and express it on Earth in our consciousness and therefore in our flesh.

If we sing out of tune the inharmony

may become so great that it may produce actual pain or even illness in a highly sensitive nature. Our bodies were originally set to music, "the music of the spheres," or the crooning of the Divine Mother, and we should and ultimately must express the theme in harmony. Our normal heart-beat gives us the measure and our breath must accord with its rhythm if we are to correlate consciously with the Great Love which gave us individuality and brought us forth, and which will ultimately bring us to perfection and at-one-ment. And since man is made in the image of God, both Divine Will and Divine Love can use the breath to bring forth, not only health of body and mind, but also oneness with our Divine Self, which is always attuned to Divine Harmony or God.

Another symbol of "the Power of the Highest and the Holy Ghost," which overshadowed Mary that the Christ might manifest is the Dove which descended upon the head of Jesus at His baptism, and the Voice which proclaimed the word: "This is my beloved Son in whom I am well pleased." Hence our Divine Parents are well pleased when the Christ-consciousness is born in us, after we have become so purified and harmonized that Divine Love can find a resting place on our heads and the Divine Wisdom has entered into our consciousness, and the Voice can speak to us within; just as an inventor is well pleased when he has perfected the mechanism of his invention and finds that it will run or respond to his guidance.

All creation is an expression of the Son or the progeny of the great creative stream of Divine Love and Will. Hence, as St. Paul tells us: "The whole creation groaneth and travaileth in pain together until now. And not only they but ourselves also, which have the first fruits of the Spirit, even we ourselves groan within ourselves, waiting for the adoption—to-wit, the redemption of our body."[*]

In other words, all Nature groans and travails in unrest until harmony and perfection are manifested, and we groan and travail in unrest until the Christ-life and consciousness finds expression through us and literally redeems our body. For until man, by correlating with the Divine Mother, has brought forth the Christ in its fullness in the Race there can be no rest in Nature, for its highest and crowning creation (man) is incomplete.

Therefore, since we have back of us the mighty urge of all evolution toward

[*] *Romans,* VIII, 22-3.

perfection, we must ultimately conquer. But if we knowingly strive to respond to the Love of the Divine Mother we can bring forth "that holy thing" which is the Christ far more quickly than when merely floating on the sluggish current of physical evolution, and can accomplish this new birth without having to pass through the suffering which ignorance and failure to work in harmony with the Divine Law necessarily entails.

MIDNIGHT PRAYER

This prayer has a dual purpose, both to bring comfort and peace whenever in-harmony or discouragement assail us, and especially to use at night when the forces of the Sun have been withdrawn and the astral forces are sweeping clos-est and having greatest power on Earth, as well as whenever we are wakeful, rest-less or apprehensive. Take a few rhythmic breaths*—say seven—until calmed and quieted, and then repeat the prayer. If cir-cumstances will permit, repeat this prayer aloud, thus voicing the consciousness and aiding us to realize the presence and the power of the Divine Mother.

O, Divine Mother! I feel Thy Love

enfolding and surging through me as it breathes and pulsates throughout the Universe.

Beloved Mother! I surrender to Thee my thoughts, my desires, my will, and rest in peace upon Thy bosom.

Let the Waters of Life cleanse and purify me.

Bring forth in me the fulness of Thy Son, the Christ.

As my consciousness is released in sleep, open for me the door of Divine Consciousness and bear me in Thine arms into the Presence of the Most High, that the Wisdom of Life may be expounded unto me.

CHAPTER II

THE BRINGER FORTH

"Isis. . . . is that part of Nature which, as feminine, contains in herself, as nurse (nutrix), all things to be born." *The Secret Doctrine*, Blavatsky, III, 154.

"Bestride the Bird of Life, if thou would'st know." *The Voice of the Silence*, Blavatsky, 5.

"The Heavenly Dove whose head is Wisdom, whose body is Humility, whose right wing is Life Immortal, and whose left wing is Divine Love—and having found this nest attain sweet rest 'between the wings of that which is not born, nor dies.'" *The Key to the Universe*, Curtiss, 328.

IN all religions we have God—the Absolute, the Causeless Cause, the great Source of all—represented as a Trinity: God-the-Father (Divine Will) God-the-Mother (Divine Love), and God-the-Son (Divine Life or the Cosmic Christ-force). This Trinity manifests in Nature as in man: God-the-Father as the formative and individualizing Consciousness which projects the ideal or pattern of that which is to manifest, the pattern within the seed, within the

egg and within man. As a Son of God man
uses this Father-force as the formulating
and projecting power of will and thought.

God-the-Mother manifests in Nature as
that which nourishes the seed; which brings
to it all the ingredients necessary for it to
unfold, bring forth and manifest the ideal
or pattern implanted by God-the-Father.
In man it feeds him with spiritual manna,
nourishes all the seeds or qualities of good
now lying dormant under the snows of "the
winter of our discontent" — even while de-
stroying in the fire of suffering all false
growth brought forth because he turned
away from the Sun of Righteousness —
that ultimately man may bring forth and
express all his God-qualities and powers
until he truly manifests as a Son of God. It
also manifests as that undying hope which
ever rises Phoenix-like from the ashes of
discouragement.

As God-the-Son is the result of the interaction of the Father-Mother-forces, in
Nature we see it manifest as the Divine
Life-force, the power back of the law of
growth, which gathers up the nourishing materials furnished by the Divine
Mother and builds them into, and thus
makes manifest, the pattern projected
by the Father. In man it is that inner

urge toward perfection; that consciousness which ultimately grasps the lessons from the experiences of life and builds them into Soul-growth, that the Real Self may ultimately manifest. It is that intelligence which enables man to work understandingly, once he has truly learned the lessons the experiences were meant to teach, in co-operation with his Divine Parents and consciously become Their representative in the manifested worlds.

The *Sepher Yetzirah* or "Book of Formation," considered to be the oldest philosophical treatise extant in the Hebrew language, teaches the existence of a single Divine Power (God) which manifests in variety and multiplicity, yet creating Unity and Harmony. The Mother-aspect of this one Divine Power is represented as a trinity by the three letters, Aleph, Mem and Shin, said to correspond to air, fire and water. The heavens or firmament, it states, was produced from fire—i.e., the Mother-aspect manifesting as the essence of Divine Life and Love, the warmth of Divine Love, the brooding of the mother bird on her nest. The earth, it says, was brought forth from water, the Mother-aspect, as the Waters of Life in which all things germinate. In our simile of the bird, the

Earth would correspond to the solid substance of the incubating eggs evolved by the coagulating and transformation of the fluids of the eggs. The Spirit is said to come forth from air "as a reconciler between them"—i.e., only the Spirit of Divinity can "reconcile" or synthesize earth, fire and water and produce warm, moist earth in which all the seeds or germs of life planted therein can bring forth.

Again, the Divine Mother-force of attraction is expressed as the trinity; heat, electricity and magnetism, or the warmth of ardent love, which is peace, harmony and cohesion; electricity—of which mankind today knows only the outer manifestation—the purging, cleansing and purifying aspect; and magnetism, which is vitality, the attracting, bringing forth and nourishing aspect of the Divine Mother. These three aspects are one, yet without their differentiation all manifestations of life and form would cease.

The understanding of the Divine Mother-force, as God bringing forth in manifestation on this plane through Love, is one of the great mysteries of God. But Jesus tells His disciples—who include all those who are sincerely trying to follow the Christ-life—"Unto you (those who have correlated with and have forsaken all to follow Him) it is given to know the mysteries of the kingdom of God." Now, if it is given us to know these mysteries, it is not only possible to grasp and understand them, but there is some definite way of arriving at a solution of their meaning now so seemingly incomprehensible. Moreover, it is our duty to make the effort to understand, for unto us it is given as a task to be performed as His disciples. This definite way is an effort, through aspiration and self-surrender, to merge our personal consciousness and understanding into the ocean of Divine Love which surrounds us, ever striving to fill us and bear us on to oneness with God. It is through Divine Love that we must open the door through which Divine Wisdom can flow.

To truly learn of God we must study the great book of Nature which God has prepared for us. Altho this book may be sealed to the understanding of the profane, it is open wide to all who approach it in reverent obedience to the guiding hand of the Divine Mother. And in it, if we realize that the same life-force we see animating Nature is also animating us, we will find that every problem is worked out. Solomon tells us: "Go to the ant, thou sluggard. Consider her ways and be wise." We are also told to consider the lilies of the field, how they grow, for by the same nourishing Love-force of the Divine Mother, out of the mire of earth-conditions, we too shall bring forth after our Divine Prototype or pattern, and blossom and reach our perfection, even as do the lilies.

If God so clothed the grass of the field in beauty, vitality and health, and supplied it with everything needed to make its life expression complete, have we not a right to expect that we, His children, the crowning point of manifested creation, shall—if we respond to and follow the same Law—find a universal supply for all our needs? Shall we not be clothed in beauty and perfection of expression surpassing as far that of the lily or the rose as man surpasses them in the scale of evolution? Shall we not be nourished and fed and abundantly supplied with all that goes to make life a continuous expression of peace, harmony, abundance and joy, even as are the lily and the rose, reflecting God's image in beauty, health and usefulness to the same extent that man exceeds the usefulness of the grass of the field?

The bringing forth of this perfected manifestation is the work of the Divine Mother-heart, for the heart of the

Mother is the Heart of the World. Only that which is true can abide there. All that is inharmonious, false or impure, having been brought forth not by Her, but by man's misuse of his God-given powers and materials, must be cast out, for the source of attraction cannot correlate with it, hence throws it out through the force of selection or repulsion.

Therefore, if we make false affirmations; if we claim that we are now manifesting the force of Eternal Life as perfect health and we have not yet reached that consciousness, or if we are working out the Karma of a body abused in a past life, or if we are not dwelling in love and correlating with the Divine Mother who nourishes us, we are asserting that which is not true, hence cannot bring it forth; for we are building on a false foundation, and every stone that is false, by the very vibrations of Divine Love, must be disintegrated and forced out of our structure.

If we make great claims as to manifesting youth, health, perfect eyesight, etc., without being able to let that consciousness manifest through us and have to go to all sorts of subterfuges to make our fellow men think we are expressing and demonstrating these things when we are not, since the vibrations of the Great

Love are steady and true and God cannot be mocked, all these things which we claim falsely must be cast out, that we may begin over again and build true and square.

We may have to age swiftly, experience illness and even die at an age when life should be surging through us abundantly. Or we may have to lose what eyesight we have that we may learn the lesson of striving for and attaining the consciousness of these things before we claim to possess them. As well might we claim to possess a gold mine or an oil well when we have only a mere "prospect."

While we are striving and seeking the true realization, the great merciful Law, like a tender mother, has provided us with many physical helps to shorten as much as possible the period needed for our schooling and to mitigate the unhappy results of our lack of realization. Thus our Divine Mother has provided for our period of ignorance, and if, like precocious children, we turn away from her gifts and refuse to use the physical helps she has provided while we are learning to unfold and manifest our higher realization of the perfection of the Real Self, we are like foolish children who refuse to have their baby teeth removed that the permanent ones may grow straight and in perfection, and we must abide by the consequences until we learn our lesson.

Many today are claiming to possess the secret of perpetual life and eternal youth, yet those who stand by and watch the results are apt to say, Why do not such demonstrate their claims? They only too often look haggard and old or negative and depleted. They make strenuous denials of physical ailments, yet they are growing hollow-eyed, wrinkled and lifeless in the effort to ignore conditions *which should be recognized and remedied.* They declare the absolute power of thought and claim that to use any physical helps, even, to wear eye-glasses, is a lack of faith, yet they either show sad marks of poor eye-sight or carry magnifying glasses to be used in private.

When Jesus was asked to heal the man who was born blind, He was asked: "Who hath sinned, this man or his parents that he was born blind?" If it was the man himself who had sinned before his birth it must have been in a previous incarnation, and as like always creates like, what more probable than that the "sin" which resulted in his being born blind might not have been the abuse of his eyes and a refusal to take proper care of them in that life?

How sad it would be if many of our well-meaning but over-eager friends who today are insisting upon doing without proper glasses before they have taken proper and scientific exercises to improve the sight, lest they be considered as "failing to demonstrate" perfect vision, and who are using their imperfect eyes without such physical helps or proper exercises when their eyes are unable to endure the strain, how sad it would be if some of them were to be born blind in their next incarnation to teach them not to refuse any of the helps toward perfection provided for them, when that lesson should have been learned here and now! Yet the parable plainly shows that even in such an event the currents of the Christ-life will ultimately extract from the experiences the new conceptions and ideas which will perfect and heal us, "that the glory of God should be made manifest."

As we enter this new Aquarian or Woman's Age, in which the down pouring of the Love of the Divine Mother is increasingly recognized, science, which has so long been looked upon as antagonistic to religion, has already demonstrated the possibility of attaining perfect vision in spite of so-called structural defects of the eye.[*] And it is making remarkable strides in other branches of healing, even tho such steps are but temporary means to help the masses until they can respond to true spiritual healing. Yet these helps are far in advance of old-time medication. The wise and loving children of the Divine Mother will, therefore, take all the gifts she holds out, knowing that the end of the journey is reached only by taking one step after the other with a thankful heart for all the blessings received along the way. We see in all these things the hand of the Divine Mother guiding us, for She does not say to the tree, "Demonstrate to me thy perfect fruit," while the tree is still but a sapling. For should a horticultural magician wave his wand and cause the immature sapling to bring forth fruit, the fruit would be ephemeral and the tree would soon wither and die.

As our Divine Mother is ever eager to gather her children into Her arms and teach them whenever they are willing to learn from Her, know well that all who are earnestly seeking the true solution of life's problems of health, happiness and abundance, shall find it when they are prepared to receive it because

---

[*] *Perfect Sight Without Glasses*, Dr. Bates.

they have learned their lessons. And be they blind or ill or in poverty, once they correlate with and surrender to and abide in that Great Love every step will bring them closer to the goal of full realization and demonstration; for every true desire awakens the force of attraction which draws to it its fulfillment.

Among the Egyptians the goddess Isis personified the Divine Mother, as Mary does with us today. Her very name means that which forever Is Is, not was or will be, but Is. "Isis as bride and mother (also as daughter), is another mystery symbolizing the Great Mother-principle in Nature and in man, which must be espoused by the Sun Initiate. In its mother aspect it gives man his spiritual birth and later, when man has made the higher correlation with it, it becomes his bride, the power through which he is able to put together, synthesize and bring forth as a god."[*] The old myth of Isis seeking and finding the body of Osiris, or the Father-aspect, broken in fourteen pieces,[**] and uniting them into one body represents the work that the Great Mother is forever doing. For as the one stream of Divine Love descends

[*] *The Secret Doctrine*, Blavatsky.
[**] *The Key of Destiny*, Curtiss, 155.

to Earth man breaks it up into many so-called loves.

Thus we speak of conjugal love, filial love, brotherly love, love of country, of home, of power, of self, etc., etc., speaking as tho each were a separate thing. But when we once sense the meaning of the Divine Mother and even for a moment are transported by the thrill of that divine ecstasy, or enter into a realization of Divine Love, all those seemingly separated pieces of the body of our Lord (manifestations of the Law) are united and we at once know that "God is Love" and that that Love fills the universe, is universal life and forever Is.

As long as man fails to realize this greatest of all truths he must continue to fail and die, for he refuses to believe in Her Son and so turns away from the stream of Divine Life. Hence he must go back into the unseen world where, unhampered by the density of Earth conditions, he can catch a glimpse of the Divine Mother and recognize Her Son as the Light of all life.

Such a person is like a child who has grown up, and having gone out into the world, repudiates the mother who bore him. For we are all spiritually born of the Mother-aspect of God, the stream of Divine Love. And our only real spiritual sustenance comes from feeding on it as it flows forth to us and to the whole universe.

Hence without Love there is no immortal life in us. We can only live out and exhaust the little store of life-force which the Divine Mother gave us at birth to carry us through this brief span of physical life. And when this is exhausted, if we fail to draw on the exhaustless supply we grow old and gradually pass away from this expression of life; for it would be cruelty to permit man to demonstrate immortality in the flesh without love. He would grow to be a monster of misery and hopeless despair, like the Wandering Jew. But the arms of the Divine Mother are held out and She is calling us back to Her bosom that once more She may suckle us at Her breast and fill us with a greater realization of Immortal Life. Then we are again sent forth to demonstrate our new lesson, wrapped round with Divine Love.

Therefore, what we call death is often a blessing, for it enables us to return to the arms of the Divine Mother more consciously, to be held close to Her heart and have new life poured into us. This is a most necessary process for the continued evolution of humanity. For, since

the majority of mankind can only realize
this Divine Love as a babe does its
mother's love and as a babe assimilates it,
and has not yet reached the development
and mental enlightenment necessary
to understand it, therefore it must be
as babes that we are sent back to the
life of physical existence with but a
vague, haunting memory of a something
wonderfully Divine which we have left,
and of something almost unattainable
which we must strive for, and an urge
which will not let us rest until, even in
our physical consciousness, we touch the
hem of the robe of Her Son and feel the
radiant Divine Life-force flow through
us. But there will come a day when we
shall "awake in his image" and shall be
satisfied, not in some future after-death
world, but here in this; the day when we
become one with the Father-Mother. This
condition once reached, we can live in
consciousness in all the worlds, even as
our Father-Mother fills all space.

Hence, whenever we call upon the
Divine Mother we feel Her presence
and know that She is near; that She has
always been near, enveloping us with
her Divine Love. It is this great Love
which is contacted and tapped through
prayers to the Divine Mother, whether

under the name of the Virgin Mary, Isis or Sakti. It is only we who have turned our backs upon Light, Love and Life. The riddle of the Sphinx is, "Man, Whence? Why? Whither?" And only through Divine Love can it be answered.

Humanity as a whole is only just now stepping into its spiritual adolescence, and the Aquarian Age (Man, the Water Bearer) marks a most important era in human evolution. In former Ages we were but babes in spiritual unfoldment, crude, cruel and unresponsive to our Divine Mother. We worshipped God-the-Father in the ignorance and pride of self-esteem, making of Him a supreme image of all that man in his selfish egotism postulated as the highest of man's attainments. We placed Him in a material heaven and cringed before Him with fear and trembling like slaves instead of Sons. Only the masculine was considered. Only the masculine side of humanity dictated the methods of His worship and approach, while woman was ignored or despised, like a stream of living water poured out upon a rock while the thirsty earth cried out for moisture, even St. Paul saying: "Let your women keep silence in the churches. . . . For the man is not of the woman; but the woman of the man. Neither was the man created for the woman; but the woman for the man."[*] This, however, but proves what we have said about true inspiration[**] —i.e., that it is not given in words, but breathed in by the Spirit. Hence, man's preconceived ideas and trend of thought and the commonly accepted ideas of his time influence his interpretation of the spiritual verities which he has sensed through inspiration, as is so evidently the case with St. Paul in his attitude toward women.

Humanity was much like a family of big, healthy boys, whose mother had passed away while they were infants and who were brought up entirely by their father and elder brother, who left them much to themselves. Yet all the time their Mother was watching over them and trying to influence them from on high, seeking in many ways to impress and guide them into the gentle arts so necessary for their complete education.

Hence often in dreams the boys would get a glimpse of their mother and their hearts would be stirred. But she seemed so far away, so unreal, that many of them could not understand that their dream had any practical bearing on their daily life, hence ridiculed, even perse-

---

[*] *I Corinthians*, XIV, 34: XI, 9-10.
[**] *The Message of Aquaria*, Curtiss, 349-50.

cuted, those whose realization was greater and who believed in their mother and sought to commune with her. Like the unseeing boys, humanity must awaken to the reality of its Divine Mother and seek to commune with Her.

Man has eaten of the Tree of the Knowledge of Good and Evil, but the Tree of Immortal Life is still guarded by the Angel with the Flaming Sword. For the Tree of Life can never yield its fruit to man until he has turned back to the Mother who bore him and has permitted Divine Love to interpret life for him.

The dawn of the New Age is upon us, yet many there be who are struggling with the sleep of the ages, still trying to live and accomplish in their own strength. How important, therefore, for us who sincerely desire to help humanity onward and upward to seek out the Divine Mother and let Her great Love fill, surround and cover us; to know Her as the Bringer-forth of our life. Only Love, unsullied by earthly misconceptions, can bring all things to our remembrance. For we do not so much learn new lessons as have brought to our remembrance the lessons given us by our Divine Mother. We touch the source of all wisdom when we recognize, correlate with and dwell in Divine Love.

Many ask, "How can I live in love when so many people are inharmonious or perhaps antagonistic to me, and the more I strive to love everyone the more inharmony I create in my life?" Such persons but reiterate the old question: "If I love not my brother whom I have seen, how can I love God whom I have not seen?" Yet there must be a way: it is this: begin by meditating on all that the Divine Mother is and means to you, and literally dwelling in that Great Love. Then realize how far all humanity has departed from it, how far you yourself have fallen short. Every time you walk out in Nature, observe the wonders of God and think how much Divine Love they express. If you see a withered leaf, a deformed tree or insect-infested growths, realize that they are all the result of man's wrong uses of his powers, by the misuse of which he has interfered with the harmonious manifestation of Divine Love.

If we would dwell close to our highest conception of Divine Love, even when our hearts are wrung by the cruel misunderstanding of earthly friends, let us lift our hands in invocation to the Divine Mother and nestle close to Her bosom until we feel the rhythmic beat of Her heart and are stilled and soothed; for She alone can enable us to realize that all that brings us closer to Her heart has ultimately worked for good. Hence, if all the misunderstanding, ingratitude and sorrow caused by our friends has taught us to turn from the outer seeming to the inner Reality for comfort, to see our faults and our own need of forgiveness and to do our own work the better, while it was not good in itself and should not have been needed by us, still it has been turned into a blessing. For only as we come to the realization that those whom we dislike are also pupils of the one Great Teacher, children of the one Divine Mother, and that they have not really harmed us, but have only in a measure delayed Her more perfect manifestation, only then are we ready for the real consecration of all we have and are and hope to be to the spread of Divine Love in humanity.

And with this realization there will also be brought home to us the realization that as long as we let our minds dwell on that which is inharmonious or on those personalities who are inharmonious with us, even if it be—as we may think—but to forgive them and wish them well, our very thinking of them is but adding to the thought of inharmony, intensifying it and tending to stir up strife; for that which we meditate upon or entertain in our minds we give power to. It is not imperfect personalities that we are to love, but the Real Self or Soul of all men and to do this we do not necessarily need to associate with inharmonious personalities.

If we have truly correlated with and realized the Love of the Divine Mother we will no longer assume a self-righteous attitude and condescendingly forgive our enemies, but will simply strive to let our Light and our newfound realization of Love shine forth, that Light and Love which radiate from us when we strive to live in Divine Love, and let them accomplish their own mission.

Realizing that our hands constitute a marvelous apparatus as specially designed to enable us to accomplish "the will of Him that sent me," if we wish to consecrate our powers to help the Divine Mother spread Her Love to humanity, we must recognize our hands as potent factors in this accomplishment. To make the correlation and consecrate our hands the following practical exercise may be used, If we wish to *receive* this force face due East; if we wish to *give out* this force face due West, and, firstly, raise the left hand and hold it, palm upward, a few inches above the head, and at the same time place the right hand over the solar plexus or pit of the stomach, and repeat the following:

INVOCATION TO THE DIVINE MOTHER

O! Divine Mother!
Illumine me with Divine Wisdom.
Vivify me with Divine Life and
Purify me with Divine Love,
That in all I think and say and do
I may be more and more Thy child.

Remain in this posture for a few seconds or until a tingling sensation in the fingers or palm of the hand shows that you have truly invoked those mysterious etheric waves of Divine Magnetism, that synthesis of all the forces of Nature, which is the expression of the Divine Mother. Then reverse the hands, lifting the right above the head and placing the left over the solar plexus and repeat the Invocation. Then, closing the eyes and shutting out every ray of light, make a mental picture of the great Bird of Life sitting close, silent and expectant upon her nest. Then imagine that you are one of her as yet unborn chicks, hence are resting in the darkness which is so necessary for the beginning of all life. Repeat to yourself, "Darkness is on the face of the deep, the deep of my Soul." Repeat this until you see and feel the darkness so pregnant with all life, and feel glowing through you the warmth of the Divine Mother, who comes to protect you with Her enfolding wings.

This is a potent and powerful mystical ceremony which should be regarded as a sacred communion with the Divine Mother and which should be performed reverently, for any flippancy or inattention or lack of sincerity will prevent results and may even cause harm.

CHAPTER III

THE WATERS OF LIFE

Holy fire from on high,
Enter in and purify.
Cleanse from dross and free from sin,
Make me pure and true within.

Stream of life unceasing flow,
Wellspring of the Christ bestow;
Fill me till I thirst no more,
Bear me to Thine eternal shore.

Hymn to the Elements,
Harriette Augusta Curtiss.

THE sign Aquarius is represented as a man pouring water out of a jar, yet this is not the kind of water which is found in the sign Pisces, the water that deluged the land at the end of the Fourth Great Race (Atlantean). Neither is it a deluge of rain, nor the hot, scalding tears of sorrow and repentance which during the Piscean Age brought peace to the Soul, nor is it the water in which the Fishes of Wisdom swim. It is not the sad tears of weeping children lost in the darkness, nor the rains and floods of disaster. All these have testified to the reign of the Piscean Age, the Age of Water.

The Age into which we are now entering is still an age of water, but the water is the Water of Life, the lifeblood of the Divine Mother, poured out through the pitcher, the symbol of the feminine side of humanity. The pitcher or ewer, or that which contains the vital Water of Life, is the Womb of the Great Mother, and this Water, which is not water but the *aqua vitae* which cannot be seen, is the synthesized power of all Nature-forces, the *akasha*, the Spirit and Soul of Ether. "Occult science recognizes seven Cosmic Elements—four entirely physical (earth, air, fire and water) and the fifth (Ether) semi-material, which will become visible in the air toward the end of our (present) Fourth Round, to reign supreme over the others during the whole of the Fifth—the remaining two are as yet absolutely beyond the range of human perception."[*] It is through this essence of the ether that the Divine Mother will manifest the power which shall bring forth in humanity the new spiritual birth for the New Age into which we have now entered.

---

[*] *The Secret Doctrine*, Blavatsky, I, 40.

While we speak of Mother Earth,[*] it should be remembered that she is the mother of our physical body only, while the Water of Life is the Divine Mother of our spiritual expression. We find this invisible downpouring of the Water of Life like liquid fire when it meets resistance or when poured upon those who are not ready to receive its baptism. How this great Mother-force, poured out from the Mother-aspect of the Godhead, clarifies, destroys and consumes! Yet as it begins to descend it is almost like dew from heaven. It falls upon the planet and upon the frightful horrors of man's wickedness like a benison of peace. Even in the midst of battle it lifts up the hearts of men to a realization that there is some great purpose back of it all, something more than human, something Divine. And upon the faces of the dying it stamps a smile of joy, as if the eyes have beholden unutterable things, things of glory unspeakable.

This awakening is not the mere awakening of the consciousness of mankind because it has suffered so intensely. It is a far greater awakening. It is the result of the pouring out upon mankind of the Water of Life. It is the baptism of the New Age poured out upon

---

(*) *The Message of Aquaria*, Curtiss, Chapter IX.

the whole world, upon the quick and the
dead, upon the Elect and upon those who
are still unenlightened and unrepentant.
How much more will it be poured out upon
those who seek to follow the Law, who
have dedicated their lives to the Divine,
who have cried out from the depths of
their hearts: "O, Almighty Power! Give us
that Divine realization, that cleansing baptism! Let us see Thy bright shining! Let
our eyes behold Thee through the clouds
of black darkness!" And the answer is,
"Verily, verily, I say unto you, those of you
who are standing fast; those of you who
have consecrated your lives as soldiers of
the Christ, who have stood in the darkness
without wavering or losing faith: Behold!
for you the Day Star is rising. Behold! for
you the great constellation Aquarius, the
Man who holds aloft the ewer of the Great
Mother, is pouring out the Waters of Life
that you may be baptized with the Holy
Ghost and with fire. As was promised by
the prophet of the past age, 'I, indeed,
baptize thee with water unto repentance:
but he that cometh after is mightier than
I. . . . he shall baptize you with the Holy
Ghost, and with fire.'"

After the devastating great flood, in
which only those who entered the Ark

of Safety in obedience to the word of the Lord were saved, after the old Karma had been washed away and the world prepared for its next great stage of development, water became to the earth its chief blessing. It so enriched the earth that it brought forth far more abundantly for man. Yet man accepted all its blessings thanklessly and turned them to many evil ends. But the water that comes from the mighty Pitcher of Aquarius is not merely to fructify Nature, but to fructify man; to fructify his spiritual nature and bring about his spiritual birth. Like the water of the Piscean Age, it begins its work for the world and humanity with a devastating baptism of fire put to its lowest uses—war. Yet when this deluge has subsided—for many of its waters and much of their debris are still with us—it will prove to be of the greatest blessing to mankind.

Everything we see in Nature has its counterpart in us. And just as the gentle baptism of rain from heaven brings up the beautiful flowers and perfects the fruits and grains, so in our hearts and lives, if we will open the doors and recognize it, will the new baptism that the Aquarian Age is pouring out fructify everything in us that corresponds to that which is fructified in

Nature by the physical water. While Nature will still put forth in greater perfection and profusion than ever before, still in every flower and fruit there will be a new potency, more force, more life, a greater beauty. Just so in our spiritual lives. Each of us will receive our baptism whether we recognize it or not, for this liquid fire which cleanses as well as fructifies wells up in each heart and in each body. But it must first purge ere it begins to beautify.

If we do not know and understand what is taking place we may become discouraged. We will think things are falling away from us; that the world is not the same; that our old joys no longer satisfy, our old companions seem to have changed. Understand and know, then, that it is the result of the new baptism. It is the Water of Life washing away and consuming all that we do not need on our Soul's journey, all that hampers our ongoing. Instead of looking outward and trying to cling to the things of the past age, look within for the little shoots that tell of the beautiful Soul-flowers that are to be, for we will soon find them, a few at first and later many.

With all our study about this most important New Age and this most important epoch of astrological events, try to realize what the passing into this Aquarian Age means to us. For just as the excessive water of the earlier Ages brought forth mighty trees, because those trees gathered from the water more than the other forms of vegetation and thus became monuments of what vegetation could accomplish, so will it be with this Water of Life of this New Age. The first fruits that will attract attention may be giant intellects, mighty hearts, great Teachers of the Race. Nevertheless, the little flowers will also spring up. Dwell on this thought and watch daily for the little shoots that are coming up, and do not trample them in the mire through ignorance or lack of care.

Perhaps our baptism will manifest only as a greater love for our fellowmen; for someone whom we have perhaps not loved before, who has seemed in some way not quite what we wanted him to be. We will wonder what has happened, why our outlook has changed. It is because the Water of Life has saturated the soil of our hearts and a flower of joy is sprouting. Perhaps we may find that when we open our lips to speak a helpful or kind word wonderful things will flow from them. We may be surprised and say, "Surely, that is not what

I intended to say! Something greater than
I was speaking through me." But it is not
so. The Water of Life has fallen upon
our hearts, has fallen upon our intellects,
has fallen upon our tongues. We have
been filled to overflowing and are simply
growing spiritually and expressing the
new lessons as blossoms of our Real Self.

CHAPTER IV

THE COMFORTER

"And I will pray the Father, and he shall give you another Comforter, that he may abide with you forever; even the Spirit of Truth; whom the world cannot receive, because it seeth him not, neither knoweth him. . . . But the Comforter, which is the Holy Ghost, whom the Father will send in my name, he shall teach you all things, and bring all things to your remembrance. . . . Nevertheless, I tell you the truth; it is expedient for you that I go away; for if I go not away, the Comforter will not come unto you." *St. John*, XII,16-26; XVI, 7.

"Earth, my Mother, bid me learn
Truth in darkness to discern.
Like thy forces, silently
Work in true humility.

Air that blows from heaven's dome,
Waft me to my Father's home.
Whisper softly words of Love
To man below from God above."

Hymn to the Elements,
Harriette Augusta Curtiss.

THE human heart yearns for comfort. Out of the hearts of humanity there arises a great longing to understand what the Holy Ghost and the Comforter can be, yet among the Gnostics and early Christians the Holy Ghost was universally regarded as the feminine Principle of the Godhead, the Divine Mother.

In the turmoil, striving and disappointments of life, as we reach out almost blindly for comfort, we are often tempted to think that it is all a dream, a beautiful vision; that either there is no Comforter or that this mystical power which the Father is to send can only come to us through great renunciation, sacrifice and crucifixion. But, in very truth, the Comforter is here now and will remain with us "even unto the end of the world." We do not realize its presence because we, like the world, cannot receive it because we see it not, neither know it.

The Comforter is, indeed, the Spirit of Truth and Love but it is more. It is the nourishing essence of the One Life, manifesting as the Mother-force or the Holy Ghost. This cosmic Mother-principle was manifested to a superlative degree through the great teacher, Jesus. Hence it was expedient for the world that He cease to focus and individualize it that we might learn to know and recognize it as the Mother-power of bringing forth in all things; that power of unfoldment which is ever tending toward perfection and ever out-growing old and worn-out conditions.

This Comforter, this divine Urge to Bring Forth, is with us as truly today as ever in the history of the world. Should it cease for one moment the entire manifested Cosmos would become dead and inert. While we should always hold the idea of Jesus as a loving teacher, helper and example, still there comes a time in each life when it is expedient for Him, as an individualized ideal, to go away; for, as He said: "If I go not away the Comforter cannot come." This means that as long as we cling to the personality of even the great Master Jesus, we are looking to an outside source for help, whereas to find the Comforter we must look within. Then we will find it not only within our own hearts, but within the heart of all things, for the Comforter or the Holy Ghost is the same outgoing divine Mother-essence of the Godhead which in the springtime enables the life-force to rejuvenate the cold, dead world into a paradise of flower and perfume and song of bird.

Only when this is understood and we realize that the great stream of Divine Love is ever near us, surrounding us and holding us fast and keeping us in all our ways, watching over us as a mother and bringing forth in us a realization of the nearness and reality of the Divine, only then are we ready to receive the Comforter. For as long as we look to the historical conception of the Teacher who walked the Earth so long ago, and look to Him alone for sustaining comfort, the Comforter, the Holy Ghost, the Divine Mother, whom He promised that the Father would send — and indeed does send to every seeking, understanding Soul — cannot contact us, for we have not opened the door of our understanding. Yet when we do open this door and enter in we will find not only the Comforter, but also Her Son, the real Jesus, as the Sun of Righteousness, waiting for us; for this little inner door opens into the "Father's house," or that state of spiritual consciousness technically called "the Kingdom of Heaven," where we will be greeted as "Sons of God" and "joint heirs with Christ." Remember, the Kingdom of Heaven is not an after-death state, but a state of spiritual consciousness to be attained here and now.*

When recognized and welcomed, this

(*) It will be extremely enlightening if students will look up all references to the Kingdom of Heaven in the New Testament, keeping the above idea in mind.

Comforter shall indeed teach us all things
and bring to our remembrance not only all
that Jesus taught, but all the great cosmic
truths which God has continually revealed
to the men of all ages through His illu-
mined seers, sages and prophets.

There is no problem in the higher life
whose solution we cannot find worked out
for us by Nature; for that which is true in
Nature is correspondingly true in man, the
microcosm. And so it is with this question.
We see the seed planted in the earth that
it may unfold its germ and enter into a
higher manifestation of life through expression. But with the Father-force of the
Sun alone it will not germinate, for it cannot sprout in dry soil. It sprouts according
to the amount of moisture (Mother-force)
in the soil. Also the Sun must "go away"
or withdraw or the seed will wither. On
the other hand, if the earth-moisture be
excessive it will rot before it germinates.
If the seed is placed in water alone it will
germinate and sprout to a certain extent,
but it will never grow and flower until
planted in the earth, just as some Souls
seem to flourish for a time on love alone,
yet can never mature without experience and understanding. But when the

seed is planted in the earth and is given a
judicious amount of moisture and a judicious amount of sunshine, there is brought
into activity, first within the earth and then
within the seed, a third element, which is
neither moisture nor sunshine, yet which
is the potent factor in growth.

It is this third force, the third person of
the Trinity, the life-potency brought into
manifestation through the action and reac-
tion of the Father-Mother forces within the
womb of Earth, by which Nature vitalizes
the seed, and by means of which the astral pattern of the future tree or flower is
unfolded and the miracle of physical manifestation and embodiment is performed.

First, there is an absorption of water and an expansion of the seed from
within, then a bursting asunder of the
husk and a little sprout puts forth. Then
tiny thread-like rootlets appear. This
pushing and expanding from within continues until a green shoot appears above
the ground and continues to grow until
it produces flower and fruit. The never
ceasing force which has produced this
miracle is neither Sun nor water, neither
Father nor Mother, but the result of the
interaction of both forces in harmony

and unity—the Son, the cosmic Christ-force.

This same miracle is wrought in humanity as each Soul, like the unsprouted seed shut up within a shell of dense, materialistic conceptions and placed in hard Earth conditions, begins to unfold through the Mother-force from within. All the forces of earthly conditions, the stern realities of life, the softening power of love and the fires of adversity, are necessary to awaken and expand the consciousness, break through the shell of former limiting conceptions and allow the Comforter to bring forth and manifest the new growth in the life.

Only as we grow, expand and receive the mystical baptism of the Holy Ghost can the Spirit of Truth within each heart send up its sprout into the higher Realms of Light, put forth its leaves, its blossoms, its fruit and become a mighty tree whose unfoldment shall furnish the birds of the air a nesting place, and whose leaves shall be for the healing of the nations.

This unfoldment of the Christ within us is due to the Comforter or Mother-force because, just as in Nature, this same Spirit of Truth unfolds an ugly and apparently dead seed into a thing of life and beauty, according to the

Truth and beauty of its astral pattern, so
are we assured that through this same cosmic Spirit we are destined to outgrow and
leave behind all the hampering conditions
and the old husks of our outgrown conceptions which so limited our outlook on
life in the earlier stages of our growth. By
dwelling in the consciousness of this inner, unseen Comforter we shall gradually
but surely absorb the Love and unfold all
our latent god-powers, even unto the perfection and flower of Christhood.

But to attain this spiritual unfoldment
there are three main stages to be passed.
The seed must first be planted in the earth.
That is we the Thinker, the I Am, must
be planted within the limitations of the
vehicle of flesh which is our representative upon Earth, and by the power of
the Christ-life within we must gradually
learn to gather up from our earthly experiences the lessons which will expand our
consciousness and soften the husk of our
personality. We will then realize that this
dark Earth condition in which we find ourselves planted is not our real home. Our
home is in the Realms of Light above the
Earth. We are only temporarily buried in
the darkness, as is the seed, that we may
put forth our roots and absorb the forces

of earth necessary to enable us to send up our sprout to function in the higher realms and unfold the flower of Christhood.

Our environment and daily duties correspond to the womb of Mother Earth. If we recognize this we will see that while they may seem dark they are really soft and warm and mellow. But ere the fructification of the Christ-seed can take place there must be a realization of the Mother-force of Divine Love and a realization of how the Father-force of Divine Wisdom, like the physical Sun, sheds its illuminating rays upon the just and unjust, its warming and vitalizing life-forces penetrating into the sorrows and heart-aches, the bitterness and poverty of Earth conditions, giving warm, sustaining power even to the unawakened seeds.

Once grasp this conception and we will see the manifestation of the Comforter everywhere around us. It is the inner Urge to Bring Forth that is ever seeking to bring into expression the inner mystical potencies—the Spirit of Truth—back of and within all life conditions. Through the manifestation of this great desire to express love, to assimilate and bring forth, the burst and outgrown husk of every seed is disintegrated, ab-

sorbed and its life-essence indrawn as
nourishment for the growing sprout, so
that as a former limitation, like a dis-
carded garment, it is soon forgotten. *Thus
shall it be with us* when we allow the
Spirit of Truth to manifest in us under all
circumstances.

Then shall every hard condition yield
up its spiritual essence or lesson and our
limitations, tribulations and sorrows shall
exist no more even as a memory, for the
Comforter has transmuted them into the
joy of the unfolding Soul-life. For just as
this same love-force tends to heal every
wound, so does it tend to heal every sorrow.
Without the tender and nourishing care of
the Comforter the Son cannot be brought
forth within us or the Christ be born in our
hearts; for the Christ-consciousness cannot be born in a heart that is as cold and
hard as a dry, unsoftened seed.

A mere intellectual conception of
this law of Nature is not enough. There
must be a manifestation. Only the baptism of the Holy Dove descending upon
the Christ-man as he stands in the river
Jordan can awaken the Spirit of Truth
within us. The instant we realize the
power of the Christ-force within us and
can say and really mean: "I can conquer. By the power of the Christ within

I can accomplish," we have prepared the soil of our minds and hearts and have sent up a ray of aspiration which shall make the descent of the Holy Ghost from heaven, like a warm spring rain, not only possible, but a reality to our consciousness.

Remember also that the actual demonstration requires a commingling of the divine potency of the two forces—the warmth of the Father and the moisture of the Mother, first the understanding, then the realization—to bring forth in the life. Both must have their manifestation within our Earth conditions; for it is that mystical force which is born of the commingling of the Sun and air with moist earth which makes the flower put forth and grow.

How hopeless, therefore, for the faint-hearted and despondent ones who really desire to grow to sit down and cry out to the Great Ones to pour out upon them as a gift something that can satisfy their heart-hunger only when developed from within! In their despair they cry out: 'Why do others receive and grow while I seem to stand still? Why has the seed beside me put up its sprout and flourished while I, with all my great desire to grow, still seem germinating within the soil? Why does God turn a deaf ear to my prayers?"

While God and the Masters and all the heavenly Hierarchies do pour out their forces of help and love, like the Sun and rain, upon us in response to our cry for Light, yet no one but ourselves can bring to us the Comforter. Remember how Simon offered money to Peter in a vain effort to obtain the gift of the Holy Ghost. Peter replied: "Thy money perish with thee, because thou hast thought that the gift of heaven may be purchased by money. Thou hast neither part nor lot in this matter; for *thy heart is not right* in the sight of God."

We cannot buy this gift. We cannot force it. *We must grow and unfold and live it*. If in our environment (the soil) we do our full duty with an aspiring heart, an open mind and some comprehension of the Law of Growth; if we permit our intellectual comprehension to bring forth in us the power to believe in ourselves — not in our weak and undeveloped lower, personal, human self, but in our Greater Self, our Real and Divine Self — we will realize that just as the evolving Christ-force in Nature extracts the life potencies from the soil, the water, air and sunshine, *so will it and must it* extract from our conditions the power to accomplish, to conquer. Only by such knowledge, faith and manifesting of the Law can we extract the Water of Life or the force of the Comforter from the baptism of the holy Ghost.

Nature drinks in this mystic Elixir of Life automatically because, being without free-will, it follows instinctively the Will of God. But man must of his own accord choose to correlate with this force. Because he is made in the image of God he must choose to let the Comforter manifest within him. For there is no such thing as coercion in the higher realms.

Man is inspired and guided toward the right path, but then is left free to exercise his power of choice and freewill. He must learn to rely upon and trust it consciously, even as Nature does instinctively, knowing that it will gradually unfold all his divine possibilities into the perfect ideal he is destined to express, just as surely as it unfolds the bud into the flower.

We are told that Solomon in all his glory was not arrayed like a lily of the field. This means that even though man attains to the wisdom of a Solomon, he cannot array his Soul in as perfect an outer expression of beauty and harmony as does the lily. Only by living calmly,

trustfully, confidently and lovingly in the
realization of the mystic glory and power
of his Real Self and permitting the force of
the Comforter to unfold the perfect pattern
can he be arrayed as the lily or manifest
the blossom of Soul perfection.

Once this is realized, the loving Master
Jesus no longer symbolizes a crucified
Saviour; for if the Comforter has gathered
into our consciousness all the mystical
lessons of the crucifixion, it has become
transmuted into our new life. We do not
need a crucified Jesus, but *a living and
glorified one*. If His disciples had watched
with Him when He was passing through
the agony of Gethsemane, He would not
have been betrayed unto death. But at the
period of development this event symbolizes the Spirit of Truth—the love for and
inner mystical comprehension of the nature of the Christ—had not been poured
out upon the disciples, hence the betrayal
and crucifixion followed.

Taking the life of Jesus to symbol-
ize the steps in the unfoldment of the
Christ consciousness in perfected man,
do we not see the above scene enacted
today in the life experience of every ad-
vancing Soul? All must some day enter
the Garden of Gethsemane and there go

apart to commune with the Father, leaving the outer faculties—the disciples and Followers—to watch, i.e., to patiently remain on guard, believing and trusting in the power of the Soul to gain the force and strength necessary to meet whatever may come. But how often they fall asleep and allow the desires of the world to enter in and betray their Christ! Three times did Jesus return and wake His disciples, saying: "Can ye not watch with me one hour?" Yet again they slept and allowed their Master to be led away to the crucifixion.

But today, if we profit by our lessons and experiences and receive the sustaining force of the Comforter, we can train all our faculties to watch that the Lord—the Law—shall not be betrayed and our Christ crucified. If any of us are now watching and praying in the Garden of Sorrow, and the power we love and trust seems for a little while to have withdrawn from us, remember this lesson.

If we watch faithfully and look toward the Mystic Light which ever shines within, there need be no betrayal or crucifixion, either of our Master, our ideals or our personality. As long as we dwell in the consciousness of the Holy Comforter, we will never slumber at the post of duty and our Lord cannot be crucified, for He is no longer a personality but an ever-living, ever-present and ever-sustaining power.

This is the Comforter which shall remain with us always "even unto the end of the world." There shall be no more doubts or sorrows, for the Comforter is within us; the Pentecostal Fire has descended upon and filled us; the five-pointed star has arisen in all its glory upon our horizon; the fifth rib has given forth its Eve and lo! a companion and helpmeet for us is forever by our side.

The ribs are a most important part of the physical frame work and serve many mystical functions. Like the arms of a loving mother, they enwrap and protect the vital organs. They are attached to the spinal column and convey the nerves from the spinal cord. In fact, they are the branches of the Tree of Life planted in the midst of the Garden; in one sense the branches of the mystic Vine to which Jesus referred when He said: "I am the Vine and ye are the branches."

The Christ-force is the life or sap of the Vine and is distributed to the branches. In the body this sap manifests as the *kundalini* force which is drawn up out of the soil of our lower nature and flows up the spinal cord—

each *chakram* or center having its own particular potency and function—until it reaches the pineal gland and ultimately opens the Third Eye. The ribs, being branches of the Tree and carrying the nerves, which are branches of the Vine, must also receive this vital sap.

Since we know this *kundalini*, or serpent power, is a dynamic, fiery force which brings either life or death when aroused, we can realize the great secret which was revealed by the symbol of Eve unfolding from the fifth rib of Adam, for it is the fifth manifestation of this fiery force which completes the evolution of the man of the Fifth Race.

Applying this symbol to the personal life, the Real Man is the Vine, while the Christ-force in him is the sap or life of the Vine. The branches are the various personalities which the Real Self puts forth in the various incarnations. It is the work of the Real Self to draw the sap of life, or the vital essence, from the alchemical laboratory of experience in Earth conditions and send it forth to all the branches, so that when He enters into oneness with the Father, He will find that all the personalities have yielded their experience.

Such branches (personalities) as refuse to allow the sap of the Christ to flow through them and bear fruit will be cut off and destroyed like the barren fig tree, i.e., will be disintegrated and their force indrawn into the Real Self, just as the disintegrating fallen branches act as fertilizer around a tree and their force is indrawn into the sap. But even tho some branches are destroyed, the tree has gathered the experience or life-essence from each, so that the fruit shall contain the potency of every branch, leaf and twig the tree has ever put forth.

Each one of us, like the disciples of old, are called to gather around a manifestation of the Christ. And just in proportion as it is possible for our faculties, forces, thoughts and aspirations to correlate with that mystic Sap of Life, just to that extent will the Vine send its vital life-force through all its ribs and branches. If we sincerely and persistently strive to dwell in the consciousness and power of the mystic Comforter, we will soon begin to see signs of growth. We will find our hearts growing more tender. We will become more patient and poised. We will find it much easier to be cheerful and joyous, to speak the kind and helpful word to everyone we meet.

Since we have recognized the Mystic Light within our Soul, our eyes have become so accustomed to it that we can see it shining in every heart, no matter how deeply veiled or covered up. Then can we feel the sorrows of others and speak the word of comfort. We will understand the reason for their unenlightenment and will strive to let our own Inner Light stream out to them and kindle their own Flame within.

When this understanding, tender sympathy and compassion manifests in our life, we may know that we have put up the first shoot that is destined to produce the Rose of Divine Love and Wisdom which is to bloom in our life and shed its spiritual fragrance abroad to all the world.

.

www.ingramcontent.com/pod-product-compliance
Lightning Source LLC
Chambersburg PA
CBHW071830020426
42331CB00007B/1680